Road Racers Revealed

Road Racers Revealed

elf2

elf2
HONDA

Alan Cathcart

Contents

Published in 1987 by Osprey Publishing Limited
27A Floral Street, London WC2E 9DP
Member company of the George Philip Group

British Library Cataloguing in Publication Data

Cathcart, Alan
    Road racers revealed.
    1. Motorcycles, Racing
    I. Title
    629.2'275   TL440
ISBN 0−85045−762−9

Editor Tony Thacker
Design Martin Richards

Typeset in Hong Kong by Setrite Typesetters
Printed in Hong Kong through Bookbuilders Ltd

Page 1
*A great moment in racing history: Sarron rounds
Spencer to take the lead in the rain at Hockenheim
in 1985 and win his first GP*

Pages 2−3
*On the right, the ELF2 'Black Bird', tested but never
raced. Opposite, the ELF2A which Le Liard raced
at the French GP in 1985*

Right
*Keeping the Italian flag flying — but with a
Japanese four-cylinder engine. The Bimota YB4
prototype clearly owes a styling debt to the Tesi*

About the author

Freelance writer Alan Cathcart is a rare combination of racer and journalist, equally able to ride, appreciate and write about the classic Grand Prix machines of yesteryear and their modern counterparts. A familiar face at factory race shops from Milan to Tokyo, and at pit garages from Silverstone to Suzuka, he has the ear of the men who build the bikes we see on the track. While others seek Eddie or Freddie or Randy or Rob for a second-hand report on the turmoil of GP race action, Alan is more likely to be prising the secrets of the bikes they race on from the machines' creators. And as one of the small band of journalists regularly permitted to test the latest in GP hardware, he is able to convey a unique inside story to the magazine readers in two dozen countries who read his articles. With a fortunate command of five different languages (sadly not yet including Japanese!), his enquiries know no frontiers, either. Yet he claims his greatest asset is an understanding wife and two children, who put up with his frequent absences abroad, on the trail of the ultimate in motorcycling exotica.

He lives in West London with his family and some historic racing motorcycles, several of which he races in classic events.

Alan Cathcart testing the 1986 Honda RVF750, featured in greater detail later in this book

Introduction

Even since I was old enough to tell a crankshaft from a camshaft, the technical aspects of motor racing on two and four wheels have fascinated me above all else. Hopelessly hooked on the sport from an early age, two decades spent on the spectators' side of the fence left me with a sense of fulfilment mixed with frustration. The sight and sound of Graham Hill fighting the wailing H16 BRM into submission, or Mike Hailwood demonstrating the art of motorcycle racing aboard the howling 297 cc Honda six were forever part of my memory bank of magic moments. But, raised as I was in the era of all-enveloping bodywork and streamlining, I longed more than anything to see what lay beneath the exterior of these marvellous machines, to gaze on the mechanical wonders cloaked by their outer skins. Such things may have been possible in the relaxed atmosphere of the Silverstone paddock in the 1960s — except I could rarely afford the cost of the infield transfer. And by the time I could, the Oriental veil of secrecy had struck, encasing them in a sea of canvas which was strictly off-limits.

Occasionally, the veil could be parted by a combination of luck and enterprise. Highlight of my personal espionage missions was the time I sneaked in the back of the Honda pit at Silverstone in 1979 and spent five whole minutes examining a spare NR500 Honda engine in minute detail, until a horrified Gerald Davison spotted my intrusion and told me to clear off in terms which would have outraged even a Honda Dealer Seminar! But it wasn't until I took the plunge in 1981 and became a full-time motorcycle journalist that I was able to start fulfilling my ambitions to discover what really makes the most exciting and avant-garde bikes in the world tick. Almost my first freelance mission was to set off on a tour of the Italian racing teams' workshops, a fruitful journey which yielded much new material and many lasting friendships. Since then, my luck in being able to persuade the leading teams and factories in motorcycle racing to allow me to test-ride their exotic, priceless machines has given me all the fulfilment I could want; not only do I get to see and discuss the bikes in minute detail, I also get to experience what they're like to ride. Sometimes I wonder if this is all a dream I am bound to wake up from one day . . . .

However, while my luck holds out, this means I've been able to get under the skin of many of the most secret and inaccessible motorcycles in the world: the factory racers. Though not all the bikes in this book qualify as such, they all have some degree of exceptional technical interest which repays long and careful scrutiny. And though a magazine racer-test article invariably carries some technical photos which permit this, there generally isn't the space or in many countries the availability of colour pages to allow lots of good, juicy close-ups to be printed. I hope this book will rectify that.

With a couple of glances over the shoulder in the form of Nessie and the Cosworth-engined bikes, the period covered in this book is mainly the 1983—86 seasons. Personally, as a student of motorcycle racing history over the decades and one who is able to appreciate the merits of bikes of all ages, I consider this to be one of the most exciting eras of technical development in the history of bike racing, on a par with the so-called 'golden ages' of 1952—57 and 1961—67. The difference is that then the emphasis was on engine design; nowadays, with a degree of conformity imposed on this aspect by the shortsighted FIM regulations, unchanged in more than a decade and a half, it is the developments in the chassis field which rivet the attention. I know that my enthusiasm for alternative forms of motorcycle design is shared by many fellow devotees all over the world, and it receives ample coverage in this volume. At the same time, the sheer variety of machines pictured inside will give the lie to the 'flat earth' attitude of so many

Indication of Bimota's influence in the Orient is provided by the Suzuki Falcorustyco, which appeared at the 1985 Tokyo Show. Apart from the hydraulic final drive, the rest of this Japanese bike is pure Tesi — hydraulic steering, opposed front swing arms, and monocoque chassis. Even the styling is a Tesi 1 rip-off, though the push-pull steering comes from the ELF2. Martini must have been flattered by the imitation

of the die-hard classic bike fraternity, who hold, for example, that because a Norton Domiracer is both old and a four-stroke, and British to boot, it must somehow be more worthy of consideration than a modern Japanese two-stroke like the NSR Honda. That view has as much foundation as trying to claim that a TD1C Yamaha is as technically exciting as a Gilera four, yet all over the world, and especially in Britain, bike enthusiasts insist on compartmentalizing their interests, instead of treating a bike on its merits. To paraphrase the US Vintage racing regulations, age and obsolescence are no guarantee of worth and nor, to turn the coin over, is modern GP racing any less exciting or technically absorbing than its

1960s counterpart. I hope the motorcycles shown in this book will support that contention.

Apart from my editor at Osprey, Tony Thacker, whose enthusiastic support when I proposed the idea of this book to him has enabled it to be put together in record time, there are many people I would like to thank for having helped to bring it about. Chief of these are, of course, the photographers I have been fortunate enough to work with on my racer tests over the past five years (and it is a fact that I have personally ridden all of the bikes pictured in this book, apart from one*): to Kel Edge, Phil Masters, Claudio Boet, Hidenobu Takeuchi and Fermino Fraternali, whose photos are, along with some of my own far more hit-and-miss efforts, included in this book, I extend my grateful thanks. And without Kay Edge, who maintains my photo and information files in apple-pie order, it would have been impossible to have assembled the book in the time available.

Yet in some ways the most important people of all are those who are accustomed to being the unsung heroes of motorcycle racing: the designers and

* Did you guess? The Suzuki Falcorustyco, of course. Does it actually run?

technicians who created and developed the bikes shown within these pages, and who took the time to talk about their ideas and engineering philosophies with me, in many cases revealing hitherto untold secrets in the process. They are the ones who made this book possible, by removing the fibreglass veil from their creations so that the camera lens could gaze upon them. So thanks most of all to Armstrong's Mike Eatough; Andre de Cortanze, Dan Trema and Serge Rosset of ELF; Bob Jarvis-Campbell, the man who rescued Nessie from drowning; the creative Antonio Cobas and Claude Fior; ace tiddler tuner, Paco Tombas of Derbi; Honda's Yoichi Oguma, Takeo Fukui and the legendary Aika-san; Jacky Germain and Kel Carruthers, respectively of the Sonauto and Agostini Yamaha teams; Nigel Leaper and Martyn Ogbourne, creators of the Heron Suzukis; the prolific and amiable Federico Martini of Bimota, also a good friend; and Rob Sewell, Ian Sutherland, Gary Flood and Bob Graves, between them the creators of the brace of Cosworth-engined machines featured in the book. To these and anyone I may have inadvertently omitted, my sincere and grateful thanks for allowing my photographers and I to get under the skin of these, their motorcycles.

A British bike leads at Daytona! Louey leads the Italian Mob, with Lucchinelli ahead of Adamo on 850 and 818 cc Ducatis respectively

Alan Cathcart
London, December 1986

Armstrong CF250

British chassis designers have long been justly applauded for their efforts on both two and four wheels. When Mike Eatough's twin-spar carbon-fibre Armstrong frame made its début at the 1983 British GP, it was seen as a breakthrough in the application of space-age material technology to motorcycle design — even if the honour of the first carbon-

Above
With a 1370 mm (54 in.) wheelbase, the Armstrong was rangy by 250-class standards. Various diameter wheels were used, though here a 16 in. front Astralite is mated to an 18 in. rear Dymag

Left
Niall Mackenzie testing the Armstrong at Oulton Park in 1985. You can see why he wears kneepads!

chassised bike, and a monocoque at that, to be raced on the tracks had already gone to the New Zealand-built TT1 Suzuki raced by Dave Hiscock in that year's Isle of Man TT.

Near bullet-proof, in spite of the attempts at destruction testing on the part of its various riders, the Armstrong achieved great strength with lightness in an impressive demonstration of the value of combining aluminium honeycomb with laid-up carbon weave. In original form it tipped the scales right on the 90 kg class limit, though the later addition of heavier forks and other components raised this slightly. But the main drawback was the need to utilize the tandem-twin Rotax engine, whereas the chassis had been developed to house Armstrong's own similar unit, designed by Barry Hart. But when Hart left the motorcycle industry, Armstrong were forced to fall back on the soon-to-be-obsolescent Rotax, whose reliability became suspect in contention with the new era of Japanese V-twins from Honda

and Yamaha. Nevertheless, riders Donnie McLeod and Niall Mackenzie dominated British 250 (and 350) class racing with the bikes, and obtained several notable GP results, with McLeod's second place in the wet 1986 Belgian GP at Spa the highest placing. In future, though, the Armstrong is likely to be best remembered as the machine which brought Niall Mackenzie to prominence and led to his works ride with Honda.

Armstrong CF250

Engine:	Twin cylinder in-line disc-valve two-stroke
Bore × stroke:	54 × 54.5 mm
Capacity:	249 cc
Output:	74 bhp at 12,500 rpm
Carburation:	Two 37 mm Dell'Orto
Ignition:	Motoplat CDI
Gearbox:	Six-speed
Clutch:	14-plate air-cooled dry
Chassis:	Twin-spar carbon fibre with aluminium honeycomb
Suspension:	Front: 40 mm Forcella Italia telescopic forks Rear: Triangular carbon-fibre swing arm with horizontally-mounted Armstrong/Öhlins damper unit working in traction
Wheelbase:	1370 mm
Brakes:	Front: Two 260 mm Brembo discs with four-piston Brembo calipers Rear: One 220 mm Brembo disc/caliper
Tyres:	Front: 3.25/4.25 × 17 in. Dunlop KR106 on Marvic wheel Rear: 3.50/5.25 × 18 in. Dunlop KR106 on Dymag wheel
Weight:	94 kg with oil/water, no fuel
Top speed:	155 mph
Year of manufacture:	1984
Owner:	Armstrong Motorcycles Ltd, Bolton, Lancashire, England

Above

As Antonio Cobas was the first to figure out, the Rotax engine's architecture lends itself ideally to the twin-spar chassis concept. By this time (1986), the team's engines were tuned by Austrian Michael Schafleitner (previously of gearbox fame); his special exhaust pipes are fitted

Right

Forcella Italia forks and Brembo brakes help to make an almost 100 per cent Euro-bike. The directional weave of the carbon strands, so crucial to the structure's strength, are evident here. Note too the double-layer radiators, for added cooling potential without extra width

Armstrong are one of the world's largest
manufacturers of suspension units for the
automotive industry, so it might have been
expected that their motorcycle would break new
ground in this field. The rear unit works in traction,
rather than the almost universal compression, for
greater rigidity and control. Note the swing arm,
also made from alloy honeycomb faced with
carbon fibre — together it and the main chassis
weigh less than 5 kg, even with all the necessary
metal inserts, bearings and steering head races.
Kevlar reinforcement is added in this area and the
fork angle is adjustable from 25 to 27 degrees by
means of eccentric metal inserts. The large knob
offers adjustable preload

ELF

Patriotically bedecked in French tricolore livery, the 1000 cc Honda TT1-engined ELFe endurance racer in its final 1983 form. Thanks to the car-type magnesium wheels front and rear, a pit stop to refuel and change both tyres could be carried out in just 12 seconds. That's the fuel tank under the engine, forming part of the wind-tunnel-developed streamlining. Thanks to the vertical steering column forming part of the hub-centre design, the riding position of the ELFe presented a novel aspect. The 'e' stood for experimental, or endurance, depending on whom you asked. Critics, however, claimed it stood for eccentric . . .

Always at the leading edge of avant-garde technology, whether introducing turbocharged engines to Formula One car racing or carbon-fibre hulls to powerboat competition, the giant French ELF petroleum company's name has become a byword for alternative motorcycle design over the past decade. Thanks to the imaginative support of ELF publicity supremo François Guiter, a series of prototypes employing such free-thinking features as chassisless construction, hub-centre steering, linked front and rear suspension, and fuel load under or beside the engine have appeared in competition, helping in so doing to push back the frontiers of accepted motorcycle design practice. Since 1980, the machines have been equipped with factory-supplied Honda engines, a recognition of the importance the world's largest motorcycle manufacturer places on the ELF project.

ELF became involved in bike racing through Guiter's friendship with Andre de Cortanze, F1 Renault racing car designer and amateur motorcycle enduro rider. Beginning with the TZ750-powered ELF X which appeared at the end of 1977, de Cortanze attempted to shatter the conventional wisdom that a motorcycle should consist of an engine fitted inside a tubular chassis equipped with telescopic forks and rear swinging fork. By 1980, ELF deemed the project sufficiently worthwhile to set up an endurance team to construct and race the 1000 cc RSC Honda-engined ELFe, which during the next three seasons was gradually developed into a high-profile, moderately-successful rolling test-bed for de Cortanze's ideas.

Left

Fuel underneath, exhausts atop. Honda tried the same idea on their first NSR500 V4 GP bike, but forgot that two-stroke exhausts are far bulkier than a neat four-into-one four-stroke system, leading to problems of heat and accessibility. Note the monoshock Marzocchi rear suspension unit placement, and cast-magnesium swing arm, later also imitated by Honda (see page 105). Those dural plates behind and above the clutch are all that remain of the chassis

Below

Twin parallel front-suspension arms were a de Cortanze trademark, with front suspension a mirror of the rear end. Brake discs are of carbon fibre and needed to be warmed to operating temperature by riding along with your hand on the lever for the first 400 metres

However, the speed at which the project could advance was hampered by the part-time nature of the designer's involvement, for by now de Cortanze had crossed to the Peugeot rally car team, where he created the 205 Turbo 16 that was to dominate the World Rally series. Nevertheless, the end of the old 1-litre TT1 formula in 1983 gave ELF the opportunity to move into GP racing, and de Cortanze to design his most way-out bike yet, the ELF2. The so-called 'Black Bird' featured a unique form of steering which, however, proved impractical in use. It was redesigned before the NS500 Honda-powered three-cylinder bike made its GP début at Le Mans in 1985, in the hands of the designer's long-time collaborator, Christian Le Liard.

The ELF2 showed a disturbing lack of awareness of the realities of GP racing, leading some to question whether de Cortanze was clairvoyant, or a charlatan. The problem most likely was that of so many forward thinkers: namely a reluctance to temper engineering ideals with pragmatism. But by now ELF wanted results as well as bikes that were different, and race

team manager Serge Rosset was deemed the man to obtain them. Under Rosset's influence and with the help of de Cortanze's deputy, Dan Trema, the bike was completely redesigned into the ELF3 which, in the hands of British rider Ron Haslam, gave ELF their first GP points in its very first race at Jarama, in 1986. Though alleged by some to have strayed too far from de Cortanze's original concept, the ELF3 was still revolutionary compared to its 500 cc class rivals, and in Haslam's hands not only finished ninth in the 1986 points table, but also handed ELF their first-ever victory in the Macau GP that year. The point had been made: alternative motorcycle design could be made to work, after all.

ELFe

Engine:	Dohc in-line four-cylinder air-cooled four-stroke
Bore × stroke:	71.6 × 62 mm
Capacity:	998 cc
Output:	128 bhp at 8000 rpm
Carburation:	Four 33 mm Keihin smooth-bores
Ignition:	Kokusan-Denki CDI
Compression ratio:	10.5:1
Gearbox:	Five-speed constant-mesh with gear primary/chain final drive
Clutch:	15-plate all-metal air-cooled dry multiplate
Chassis:	Engine used as fully-stressed member, with front and rear suspension bolted on via dural plates
Suspension:	Front: Centre hub steering with remote pivots and twin suspension arms. Single Marzocchi gas unit Rear: Single-sided swing arm with single Marzocchi gas unit
Brakes:	Front: One 300 mm SEP carbon-fibre disc with Lockheed four-piston caliper Rear: One 260 mm SEP carbon-fibre disc with Golden Brembo caliper
Tyres:	Front: 4.50 × 18 in. Dunlop slick Rear: 3.75/6.50 × 18 in. Dunlop KR133 slick
Weight:	173 kg with oil/no fuel including lights
Top speed:	178 mph (287 km/h)
Year of manufacture:	1982
Owner:	Société ELF-France, Paris, France

Left
Instead of the ELFe's vertical steering column, the ELF2 employed a unique lever steering design which required the rider to pull and push the handlebars back and forth along the axis of the wheelbase. This made it near-impossible to move around on the bike, as dictated by latter-day riding practice, and would have made push-starting it in the midst of a crowded grid difficult, if not impossible! What looks like part of the fairing is, in fact, the plastic fuel tank

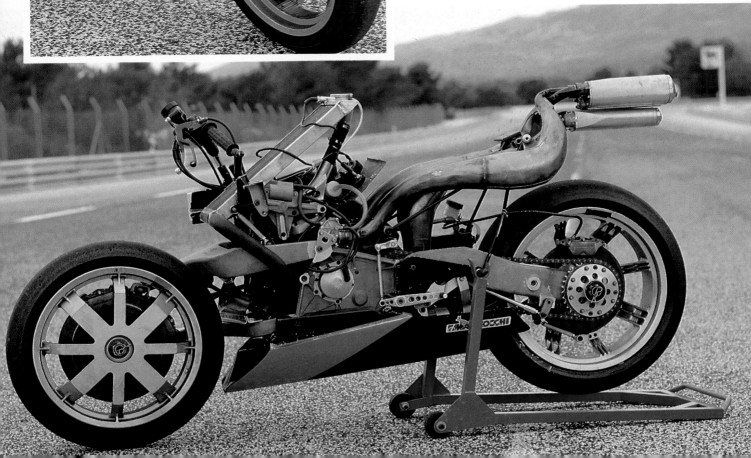

Left
By recasting the NS500 Honda engine's side covers in magnesium, de Cortanze was able to adapt the unit to his chassisless concept. Twin front swing arms are retained, but instead of the one-sided wheels both facing the same way as on the ELFe, they are now mirror-imaged. The radiator location, surprisingly, did not inconvenience the rider. Suspension units front and rear lie under the engine and work in traction

Above
ELF2A (foreground) and ELF2 — two variations on the same theme

Left
ELF2A's bodywork found an echo in the screenless Ducati Paso. Its riding position placed the rider far forward over the front wheel and was very cramped

Right
ELF2A reverted to ELFe-type steering design with abbreviated column, but otherwise was a developed version of the ELF2 'Black Bird'

Below
Because the close proximity of pivot points for front and rear swing arms induced pitching, de Cortanze introduced a car-type anti-roll bar on the ELF2A, controlled by torsion bars whose diameter could be varied to offer greater or lesser resistance. In spite of minimalist engineering, the bike was still heavy at 128 kg — 14 kg more than Honda's best factory effort with the same engine but a conventional chassis

Though outwardly similar to previous ELF designs, the Rosset-inspired ELF3 was in fact a big departure from normal de Cortanze practice

Above
The ultra-short wheelbase of ELF2 is apparent here — only 1350 mm (53 in.). Directional stability was a problem at almost any speed. The ELF2A handled better, but was no match for the conventional NS500 Honda

Left
Dan Trema (left) and Serge Rosset with the ELF3. Note the conventional alloy chassis, but MacPherson strut-inspired front suspension, with twin articulated triangles controlled by the specially-built suspension unit. A single parallel swing arm simply assures wheel location. The shrouded position of the 320 mm diameter front steel brake disc caused heat build-up which led to braking problems, in spite of the two four-piston Brembo calipers fitted

Right

The VGC (Variation Géométrique Contrôlée) front end was an alternative form of alternative suspension design

Below

Forward-facing carburettors of the V3 Honda engine prevented traditional hub-centre design, as on the ELFe. This is the ELF2C, a further development of (paradoxically) the ELF3, which combined Rosset's compromise VGC front end with de Cortanze's twin parallel front swing arms — the upper albeit in vestigial form. Débuted by Le Liard in practice at the San Marino GP in 1986, it displayed front wheel patter of truly terrifying proportions

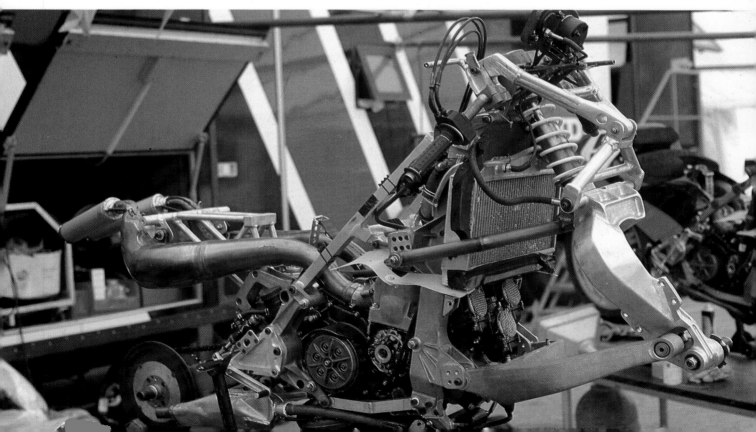

Above
The ELF2C featured a cast-magnesium front frame section for the first time in an effort to combine greater rigidity with weight saving. Note how the front suspension upright is nevertheless hand-carved from the solid

Above right
At the end of the day, the ELF3's satisfying progress during 1986 was as much due to the brilliant development talents and brave riding of Ron Haslam as to anything else. At least it persuaded Honda to supply new-type NSR V4 engines for 1987 — and the ELF4

ELF2 and ELF2A

Engine:	Water-cooled reed-valve 90-degree V3 two-stroke
Bore × stroke:	62.6 × 54 mm
Capacity:	499 cc
Output:	128 bhp at 11,500 rpm
Carburation:	Three 37 mm eliptical-choke Keihin
Ignition:	Kokusan-Denki CDI
Gearbox:	Six-speed
Clutch:	Multiplate dry (seven friction/seven steel)
Chassis:	None as such — front and rear suspension bolted to specially-cast magnesium engine side covers, employing engine as chassis
Suspension:	Front: Twin parallel swing arms employing rod and shaft steering (ELF2) or vertical-column steering (ELF2A), with monoshock suspension employing Marzocchi unit working in traction (ELF2) or compression (ELF2A) Rear: Single-sided cast-magnesium swing arm with Marzocchi suspension unit working in traction (both bikes), located horizontally under engine and offering full rising rate
Wheelbase:	1350 mm (ELF2); 1390 mm (ELF2A)
Brakes:	Front: One 300 mm SEP carbon-fibre disc with two four-piston Brembo calipers Rear: One 300 mm carbon-fibre SEP disc with single four-piston Brembo caliper
Tyres:	Front: 3.75/4.25 × 17 in. Dunlop cross-ply on 3.5 in. cast-magnesium wheel Rear: 3.70/7.20 × 18 in. Dunlop radial on 5 in. cast-magnesium wheel
Weight:	137 kg with oil/water (ELF2); 128 kg with oil/water (ELF2A)
Top speed:	Approx. 290 km/h
Year of manufacture:	1984 (ELF2); 1985 (ELF2A)
Owner:	Société ELF-France, Paris, France

ELF3

Engine:	Water-cooled reed valve 90-degree V3 two-stroke
Bore × stroke:	62.6 × 54 mm
Capacity:	499 cc
Output:	128 bhp at 11,500 rpm
Carburation:	Three 37 mm eliptical-choke Keihin
Ignition:	Kokusan-Denki CDI
Gearbox:	Six-speed
Clutch:	Multiplate dry (seven friction/seven steel)
Chassis:	Square-section tubular alloy abbreviated twin-loop design, also manufactured in cast magnesium
Suspension:	Front: VGC system comprising twin articulated triangles, fabricated in aluminium, operating White Power/ELF monoshock suspension unit with single horizontal steering arm
	Rear: Single swing arm with monoshock rising-rate linkage operating vertically-mounted WP/ELF unit
Wheelbase:	1455 mm
Brakes:	Front: One 320 mm cast-iron ventilated disc with two four-piston Brembo calipers
	Rear: One 300 mm carbon-fibre SEP disc with two-piston caliper
Tyres:	Front: 3.25/4.50 × 17 in. Dunlop cross-ply
	Rear: 3.70/7.20 × 18 in. Dunlop radial
Weight:	119 kg with oil/water
Weight distribution:	55/45 per cent
Top speed:	290 km/h
Year of manufacture:	1986
Owner:	Société ELF-France, Paris, France

'Nessie'

Though never remotely as well publicized or funded as the high-profile ELF effort, the first chink in the curtain of convention enveloping motorcycle chassis design during the modern era was in fact poked through by a team of British amateurs taking part in mid-1970s endurance events: Mike Tomkinson and his sons Chris and Patrick, and their collaborator Jack Difazio.

After surprising many with the speed and reliability of their single-cylinder BSA Victor in the early 1970s, the Mead and Tomkinson équipe turned to multi-cylinder machinery with a hub-centre Laverda triple housed in a Difazio chassis. This in turn led to the immortal 'Nessie', a Z1 Kawasaki-engined device which by the time de Cortanze's first design, the ELF X, appeared at the 1977 Paris Salon, had already raced and scored an FIM championship point.

Thus christened by, ironically, a French friend on account of its grotesque appearance, Nessie was empirically developed in endurance races thereafter until the Tomkinsons retired from racing at the end of 1981. Of similar layout to the later ELFe, which aped many of its then-unique features, such as one-sided rear suspension, car-type wheels, fuel under the engine and exhausts on top, Nessie's steering system was idiosyncratic since, in an effort to reduce the long trail inherent in hub-centre designs, the Tomkinsons placed a kingpin inside the hub and located the axle on trailing links. The use of light-weight steel tubing kept unsprung and overall weight to a minimum, though handling was sometimes unpredictable and brake pad knock-off a problem.

After Nessie retired from the endurance world, she was bought by British enthusiast Bob Jarvis-Campbell, who initially rode her on the road before planning a return to the tracks with a modified version, effectively continuing the Tomkinsons' line of development.

Left
The similarity to the later ELFe is pronounced (see page 17). Forward location of front brake caliper made pad knock-off a problem

Above
The swinging fork simply positions the wheel in space and carries no vertical loading. Though not visible, the kingpin is mounted inside the hub, with a short alloy extension through which the main axle passes; this is slightly offset to offer the same degree of lock in both directions, thus overcoming one of the parallel swing-arm ELF design's biggest disadvantages

Below
Nessie at speed round the Mallory lake in 1986. Handling was 'interesting', to say the least — sometimes it seemed she wanted to take a dip in the water . . . . The Loch Ness Monster had become the Great White Whale!

Right
Bob Jarvis-Campbell explains Nessie's front-end design. The black fibreglass cover houses the belt drive to the Citroën 2CV alternator

Mead & Tomkinson Kawasaki 'Nessie'

Engine:	Dohc air-cooled tranverse in-line four-cylinder four-stroke		Rear: Single swing arm monoshock with single De Carbon unit
Bore × stroke:	69 × 66 mm	Wheelbase:	1475 mm
Capacity:	984 cc	Brakes:	Front: Two 11 in. Hunt alloy discs with Lockheed calipers
Output:	110 bhp at 9000 rpm		Rear: One 240 mm Brembo cast-iron disc with Lockheed caliper
Carburation:	Four 31 mm Keihin smooth-bores		
Ignition:	Lucas Rita electronic with belt-driven Citroën generator and 12-volt battery	Tyres:	Front: 3.25/3.50 × 18 in. Dunlop KR108 hand-cut slick on 2.5 in. wire wheel
			Rear: 3.50/6.50 × 18 in. Dunlop KR135 hand-cut slick on 4 in. Peter Williams magalloy wheel
Gearbox:	Five-speed Yoshimura close-ratio		
Clutch:	Multiplate oilbath		
Chassis:	Engine employed as fully stressed member, with front and rear suspension bolted directly thereto	Weight:	183 kg with oil, no fuel (in endurance form)
		Top speed:	165 mph
Suspension:	Front: Centre hub steering with trailing link axle location and twin wishbone suspension, and single De Carbon unit	Year of manufacture:	1977
		Owner:	Robert Jarvis-Campbell, Enfield, Middlesex, England

Cobas—or Kobas

Few current designers are as prolific as Spaniard Antonio Cobas — really only Britain's Steve and Lester Harris approach him in range and versatility. Moreover, Cobas is an innovator, earning most recognition for being the originator of the twin-spar chassis now commonplace in GP racing; whether you call it a Deltabox or a Diamond frame, the fact is that the concept was first displayed on the Kobas-Rotax 250 of 1981. Why with a 'K'? Because the guy designing the tank badge thought it looked neater that way, is why!

The Kobas brought the work of this young Spanish designer to the world stage, though previously he had already built and sold around 100 spaceframe Siroko chassis for Yamaha and Rotax 250s. It also brought Sito Pons and Carlos Cardus to the forefront, then more recently Juan Garriga, and proved Spain to be a rich source of rider talent for Japanese and other factories. Though Cardus' 1983 European 250 title on a Kobas was the breakthrough for the Barcelona-built bikes, it was Pons' stirring victory in his home Spanish GP the next season on a similar machine which proved the validity of Cobas' designs.

Although, under the patronage of local sponsor Jacinto 'JJ' Moriana, Cobas has tended to concentrate on the 250 GP class, his talents have been

Left

Expatriate American Dennis Noyes really going
for it on the one-off Tecfar-Ducati 900, on which
Carlos Cardus terrorized the big Japanese fours in
Spanish superbike racing in 1982. Commissioned
by local Ducati-importer Ricardo Fargas (Tecfar =
TECnakit FARgas), this featured monoshock rising-
rate rear suspension — termed 'variable flexibility'
by Cobas — obtained by actually extending the
already rangy wheelbase to 1560 mm (61.5 in.).
Coupled with a lowered steering head and
revised steering geometry, this speeded up the
steering and permitted use to be made of the extra
ground clearance obtained by fitting wider tyres.
Cobas spaceframe was in chrome-moly tubing

Below

The 1000 cc Cobas-Yoshimura Suzuki produced
for endurance racers Toni Lasheras and Ignacio
Bulto (son of the Bultaco founder) led the 1985
Barcelona 24 Horas from the start before its
engine proved unreliable. Reducing the polar
moment of inertia by concentrating the centre of
mass and centre of gravity is a key feature of
Cobas designs — almost visually evident here.
Front end comes from an RG500 Suzuki

applied not only to Yamaha and Rotax twin-cylinder engines, but to both types of Ducati V-twin, Rotax 125, 250 KTM and 80 cc Autisa and Huvo singles, 1-litre Suzuki fours and even the unlikely BMW K100 'Flying Brick'. Never afraid to experiment, he has lately concentrated on well-triangulated tubular steel spaceframes, which offer a robust yet easily repairable vehicle for his avant-garde rear suspension designs. Hopefully, his talents will find expression on the street bike scene in the future.

A second Cobas variation on the Ducati theme was the Pantah-engined Tecfar 750, seen here in its 1984 guise when owned briefly by Spanish Ducati aficionado Falo Fernandez. Built for the 24 Horas, it achieved more success as a works bike in the Bologna factory team, Juan Garriga qualifying it on pole for the 1985 World F1 round at Montjuich and leading Dunlop's works Honda for several laps before being involved in a multi-bike accident on oil. Thereafter it was ridden with success in Italian endurance races and the BoTT at Daytona in 1986 by Stefano Caracchi. Its main advantage over the Verlicchi cantilever frame is superior rear suspension design, offering full rising rate

Stefano Caracchi in the 1986 Daytona BoTT race on the Tecfar 750, now run as a factory bike. He finished fifth after running low on fuel

Left

Carlos Cardus' 1983 Kobas Eurotitle-winner. The seminal alloy U-frame carried a 16 in. front wheel and 18 in. rear, with the already ideally-designed tandem-twin Rotax engine. Cobas was also the progenitor of the trend towards extreme front-end weight bias; on the Kobas, this was 55/45 per cent with Cardus aboard

Kobas 250

Engine:	360-degree twin-cylinder in-line disc-valve two-stroke
Bore × stroke:	54 × 54 mm
Capacity:	247 cc
Output:	72 bhp at 13,200 rpm
Carburation:	Two 37.5 mm Dell'Orto
Ignition:	Motoplat CDI
Clutch:	14-plate air-cooled dry
Chassis:	U-frame alloy construction semi-monocoque
Suspension:	Front: 35 mm Yamaha telescopic forks
	Rear: Monoshock swing arm
Wheelbase:	1395 mm
Brakes:	Front: Two 240 mm Brembo discs (floating)
	Rear: One 220 mm Brembo disc (fixed)
Tyres:	Front: 12/60 × 16 in. Michelin slick
	Rear: 14/68 × 18 in. Michelin slick
Weight:	97 kg with oil/water, no fuel
Top speed:	152 mph
Year of manufacture:	1982–83
Owner:	Jacinto Moriana, Barcelona, Spain

Above

A spaceframe Cobas-designed Siroko with 250 cc Rotax engine, dating from 1981 and fitted with 18 in. wheels. Compare this bike with the later TR2 JJ-Cobas on page 42

Right

The legendary Angel Nieto, '12 plus one'-times world champion, rode both Siroko and Kobas machines in the 250 class. Here he is seen at Daytona in 1984, as part of a three-pronged Kobas offensive that saw Pons, Cardus and Nieto qualify at the head of the field but retire in the 100-mile race. Note the extreme forward riding position, helping to achieve front-end weight bias

Two Cobi in confrontation. Right is the KTM-powered bike, with the TR2 Rotax on the left

Right
The TR2 Cobas possessed ultra-nimble steering, but required great concentration to ride hard. White Power forks were superb

Above
Budget high-tech racer for the common man. Cobas transferred his GP chassis technology to single-cylinder racing using a 250 KTM motocross engine and extruded alloy frame spars. The result cleaned up in local events

Below
Cobas moved to a steel spaceframe in 1983, citing ease of repair after accidents as the main cause. This is the ultimate development of the TR2 Rotax line, Alan Carter's 1986 GP bike. By now, 16 in. wheels are fitted at both ends, together with White Power suspension, including the evolutionary 'upside down' forks

JJ-Cobas Rotax TR2

Engine:	Water-cooled disc-valve 360-degree tandem-twin cylinder two-stroke
Bore × stroke:	54 × 54.5 mm
Capacity:	250 cc
Output:	76 bhp at 13,200 rpm (at gearbox)
Carburation:	Two 38 mm Dell'Orto
Ignition:	Motoplat CDI
Gearbox:	Six-speed
Clutch:	Multiplate dry
Chassis:	Tubular spaceframe in chrome-moly steel
Suspension:	Front: 54 mm White Power inverted telescopic forks Rear: Rising-rate monoshock with alloy swing arm and White Power unit
Wheelbase:	1340 mm
Steering head angle:	26.5 degrees
Brakes:	Front: One 320 mm Brembo disc with four-piston Brembo caliper Rear: One 180 mm Zanzani disc with two-piston Brembo caliper
Tyres:	Front: 12/60 × 16 in. Michelin on Marvic wheel Rear: 15/61 × 16 in. Michelin on Marvic wheel
Weight:	91.5 kg with oil/water, no fuel
Weight distribution:	57/43 per cent static
Top speed:	257 km/h
Year of manufacture:	1986
Owner:	Jacinto Moriana, Barcelona, Spain

Perhaps Cobas' unlikeliest race design, the brace of K100 BMW endurance racers sit slightly forlornly in the paddock before the 1984 Montjuich 24 Horas. Ignition problems caused by the computerized electronic system resulted in a poor showing, leading to immediate factory assistance where none had been previously

forthcoming. In turn, this led to a clean sweep in the Spanish superbike championship for Carlos Cardus. Standard swing arm and drive shaft are retained, enough to handle the 122 bhp wrung from the long-stroke engine by ex-Ossa technician Eduardo Giró. Front end is RG500 Suzuki again

JJ-Cobas BMW K100R

Engine:	Dohc water-cooled four-cylinder four-stroke		Rear: Single swing arm with De Carbon suspension unit
Bore × stroke:	67 × 70 mm	Wheelbase:	1440 mm
Capacity:	988 cc	Brakes:	Front: Two 300 mm Brembo floating discs with four-piston Brembo calipers
Output:	122 bhp at 9400 rpm		
Carburation:	Bosch electronic fuel injection		
Ignition:	Bosch electronic		Rear: One 280 mm BMW disc with Brembo caliper
Compression ratio:	11:1		
Gearbox:	Five-speed	Tyres:	Front: 12/60 × 16 in. Michelin on Marvic wheel
Clutch:	Single-plate diaphragm		
Chassis:	Steel tubular spaceframe with engine as stressed member		Rear: 18/72 × 18 in. Michelin on Marvic wheel
Suspension:	Front: 40 mm Kayaba telescopic forks with hydraulic anti-dive	Weight:	179 kg dry
		Top speed:	278 km/h (estimated)
		Year of manufacture:	1984
		Owner:	Jacinto Moriana, Barcelona, Spain

Fior

Above

The Fior-Honda RS500 naked. Note the triple Fior-made alloy water radiators, and Fournalès compressed-air suspension unit behind the steering head. This design eliminates fork stiction and deflection and assures constant wheelbase and trail under braking for more controllable handling

Overleaf

On a warm summer evening in Gascony, the brace of Fiors pose on the Nogaro track. The 250 Yamaha version on the right especially shows the extreme, 20-degree fork angle and forward weight distribution favoured by Fior: 60/40 per cent compared to the Honda's (left) 54/46 per cent — both static, without rider. Yet at the same time, the bikes are tall and short; seat height on the Honda is 850 mm (over 33 in.) and wheelbase 1280 mm (50.3 in.) — incredibly short for a 500

Former endurance racer Claude Fior comes from the Gascogne region of southern France, and like d'Artagnan and the Three Musketeers who also hailed from there, he is an independently-minded free spirit. Instead of the rapier, however, his chosen foil is the series of wishbone-forked GP motorcycles he has built since turning to chassis construction in 1979.

From his base at the Nogaro race circuit, Fior has constructed an evolutionary series of revolutionary bikes, at first powered by the RG500 Suzuki engine, but latterly by the three-cylinder Honda RS unit. Between times, he ekes a living making alloy fabrications for the four-wheeled racing fraternity, as well as building good-looking frames for the Bimota-class Boxer street bikes. These, however, do not follow the extreme design parameters of Fior's race bikes, which feature a fabricated alloy wishbone front fork, ultra far-forward weight distribution, an intentionally high centre of gravity, Fournalès compressed-air suspension units, and very steep fork angle. Monocoque chassis design was a feature of the last Fior-Suzuki, but this was dropped on the grounds of cost and ease of repair. Instead, on the RS Hondas and the subsequent Fior-Yamaha TZ250, his first excursion into the smaller class, a light but strong tubular alloy frame is used.

Left
After Gentile wrote off a frame in an early-season crash in 1986, Fior produced a revised version of the design which featured a broader lower pivot to spread the loads more evenly. The chassis was also beefed up, at the cost of 2 kg overall weight increase, but at 119 kg the Fior was still easily the lightest production-engined Honda triple

Above left
Close-up of the Honda front end. The fork is effectively a racing car suspension wishbone turned through 90 degrees. Hossack in Britain and Parker in the USA utilize similar designs

Left
The short wheelbase and high centre of gravity make the Fior-Honda hard to get used to, with wheelies a constant factor even when hitting a bump cranked over. But the braking potential is phenomenal and manoeuvrability in tight corners excellent

Fior-Honda RS500

Engine:	90-degree V3 reed-valve water-cooled two-stroke with twin ATAC
Bore × stroke:	62.6 × 54 mm
Capacity:	499 cc
Output:	125 bhp at 11,500 rpm
Carburation:	Three 36 mm Keihin
Ignition:	Kokusan-Denki CDI
Gearbox:	Six-speed
Clutch:	14-plate dry (seven friction/seven steel)
Chassis:	Twin-loop square-section aluminium tubular
Suspension:	Front: Fabricated alloy wishbone with Fournalès compressed-air unit Rear: Box-section alloy swing arm with Fior rocker-arm suspension and single Fournalès unit
Wheelbase:	1280 mm
Steering head angle:	24 degrees
Brakes:	Front: Two 280 mm floating Brembo discs with four-piston calipers Rear: One 220 mm fixed Brembo disc with two-piston caliper
Tyres:	Front: 12/60 × 16 in. Michelin slick on Marvic wheel Rear: 18/67 × 16 in. Michelin slick on Marvic wheel
Weight:	117 kg with oil/water, no fuel
Top speed:	285 km/h
Year of manufacture:	1984
Owner:	Claude Fior, Nogaro, France

That the designs work well is shown by European champion Marco Gentile's consistent placings at the head of the real privateers in the 1986 GPs — three 11th places just behind the NS-powered ELF3, on a fraction of the available budget. One wonders what Fior might have achieved had ELF decided to subsidize his particular form of Gallic alternative design, rather than that of Andre de Cortanze.

Above
The Fior 250 used the same wheelbase as the 500, but with steeper fork angle and more weight on the front wheel. The placement of the twin Fournalès units is especially neat

Right
Claude Fior (with moustache) is an excellent test rider for his own designs. Here he sorts out the TZ250 for regular rider Marc Gual

Above

Fior contends that the most desirable position for the centre of gravity on a motorcycle is just behind a position directly above the front wheel, so that

under braking it shifts to a point directly above the contact patch and pushes the wheel on to the tarmac. He calls this the 'wheelbarrow principle'!

Fior-Yamaha TZ250

Engine:	Parallel twin-cylinder reed-valve water-cooled two-stroke without exhaust valve		with Fior cantilever suspension and single Fournalès unit
Bore × stroke:	56 × 50.7 mm	*Wheelbase:*	1280 mm
Capacity:	249 cc	*Steering head angle:*	20 degrees
Output:	65 bhp at 12,500 rpm (estimated)	*Brakes:*	Front: One 280 mm floating Brembo disc with four-piston caliper
Carburation:	Two 36 mm Mikuni		
Ignition:	CDI		Rear: One 220 mm fixed Brembo disc with twin-piston caliper
Gearbox:	Six-speed		
Clutch:	11-plate dry (five friction/six steel)	*Tyres:*	Front: 12/60 × 16 in. Michelin slick on Campagnolo wheel
Chassis:	Twin-loop square-section aluminium tubular		Rear: 14/68 × 18 in. Michelin slick on Campagnolo wheel
Suspension:	Front: Fabricated alloy wishbone with Fournalès unit	*Weight:*	91 kg with oil/water, no fuel
		Top speed:	240 km/h
	Rear: Fabricated alloy swing arm	*Year of manufacture:*	1985
		Owner:	Claude Fior, Nogaro, France

Derbi 80

Everything is relative. Aspar's 1984 works Derbis may look low and long, but at 1280 mm wheelbase they are small-scale replicas of a larger GP bike. The bike on the left has 32 mm Marzocchi forks used throughout the season, while the one on the right is an experimental version with Forcella Italias

Winners of five world titles in the 50 and 125 cc classes in the early 1970s, the Spanish Derbi factory were initially at the forefront of small-capacity GP racing after the introduction of the current FIM rules in 1969, which effectively banned the multi-cylinder Japanese machines.

After this success, Derbi took a back seat internationally for a decade while concentrating on development of their road bike and MX business. They returned to GP racing in 1984 in the newly-introduced 80 cc class, and two years later achieved their goal of a further world title, thanks to the riding skills of Jorge Martinez, nicknamed 'Aspar', who was able to fend off determined challenges not only from the works Krauser, Seel, Autisa and Casal teams, but also from his team-mates Herrero and Nieto.

During Derbi's ten-year absence from GP racing, the 'tiddler' class had evolved from a cottage industry

Above

The 1984 machine embodied an alloy monocoque chassis for Derbi's return to GP racing. Riders claimed it lacked 'feel' and was unpredictable in handling. It was also heavy; at 60.5 kg dry, the bike was 5 kg over its class weight limit, partially due also to the copper radiator fitted mid-season to cure mid-race overheating, leading to power fall-off

Above right

The 1984 Derbi also featured a twin-shock rear end using Bitubo units, and Kawasaki/Garelli-type mechanical front anti-dive, pioneered on the Geitl/Schuster BMW Superbike in the USA during the mid-1970s. That foam rubber shroud helps to isolate the 32 mm Dell'Orto carb from radiator heat

1984 Derbi 80

Engine:	Single-cylinder disc-valve water-cooled two-stroke
Bore × stroke:	48 × 44 mm
Capacity:	79.80 cc
Output:	28 bhp at 14,500 rpm
Carburation:	32 or 34 mm Dell'Orto
Ignition:	Motoplat CDI
Gearbox:	Six-speed
Clutch:	12-plate dry (six metal/six fibre)
Chassis:	Full alloy monocoque
Suspension:	Front: 32 mm Marzocchi telescopic forks with mechanical anti-dive Rear: Swinging arm with twin Bitubo suspension units and mechanical anti-squat
Wheelbase:	1280 mm
Brakes:	Front: Two 220 mm Zanzani discs with Brembo calipers Rear: One 200 mm Zanzani disc with Brembo caliper
Tyres:	Front: 7/54 × 16 in. Michelin slick on Campagnolo wheel Rear: 8/61 × 18 in. Michelin slick on Campagnolo wheel
Weight:	60.5 kg dry
Top speed:	220 km/h
Year of manufacture:	1984
Owner:	Derbi, Nacional Motor SA, Barcelona, Spain

to a race for miniaturized versions of the bigger GP bikes that in some ways surpassed their big brothers in high-tech design and sophistication. In a motorcycle weighing less than 60 kg, 30 bhp gave startling performance, and new-generation tyres ensured cornering speeds as high as, if not higher than, the bigger GP bikes. The difference is that with engines of this size, gains are measured in fractions of a bhp, rather than several additional horsepower — and chassis design and streamlining become even more important.

Left
Aspar waiting in the warm-up area for the start of the 1985 Spanish GP. He won. By now, the monocoque has given way to the tubular steel spaceframe which in due course won the 1986 world title

Below
The 1986 world champion Derbi. The degree of evolution in just two years is remarkable, compared to the photo on page 54. The power unit is smaller and lighter, yet yields an extra 2 bhp; the radiator is now alloy and its chassis is the tubular spaceframe introduced in 1985, with more modern White Power rising-rate rear end. In spite of an extra 1.5 kg penalty inflicted for 'upside down' WP forks, the weight is down to 59 kg — only four more to go! Carb size is up to 35 mm for fast circuits, though the slight weight penalty of the alloy Dell'Orto is accepted due to the inexplicable habit of a magnesium-bodied one to suddenly stop delivering mixture, leading to inevitable seizure. The use of a wet-cell battery to power the Motoplat ignition is surprising, in view of lightweight solid-state models that are available. Nose fairing and seat are crucial parts of wind-tunnel-developed streamlining

If the major Japanese factories should return in the future to contest the new single-cylinder 125 class, it's likely that they will find the accumulated experience in small-capacity GP development of European teams like Derbi, Garelli, MBA and Krauser a hard nut to crack. Meanwhile, the Derbi establishes a benchmark for miniaturized GP design.

Below
Aspar winning the 1985 Spanish GP en route to runner-up slot in the world championship. The following year, he'd go one better

Right
A massive magnesium clutch housing dominates the right side of this Derbi engine. Development chief Paco Tombas was responsible for startling performance from an 80 cc unit. Note the well-triangulated chrome-moly frame

1986 Derbi 80

Engine:	Single-cylinder disc-valve water-cooled two-stroke
Bore × stroke:	48 × 44 mm
Capacity:	79.80 cc
Output:	29.9 bhp at 14,500 rpm
Carburation:	One 34 mm or 35 mm Dell'Orto
Ignition:	Motoplat CDI
Compression ratio:	14:1
Gearbox:	Six-speed
Clutch:	12-plate dry (six metal/six fibre)
Chassis:	Chrome-moly tubular spaceframe
Suspension:	Front: 54 mm White Power inverted telescopic forks with 40 mm sliders
	Rear: Monoshock swing arm with single White Power unit
Wheelbase:	1300 mm
Steering head angle:	26 or 26.5 degrees
Brakes:	Front: Two 220 mm Zanzani discs with Brembo calipers
	Rear: One 200 mm Zanzani disc with Brembo caliper
Tyres:	Front: 7/54 × 16 in. Michelin slick on Marvic wheel
	Rear: 8/61 × 18 in. Michelin slick on Marvic wheel
Weight:	59 kg dry
Top speed:	225 km/h
Year of manufacture:	1986
Owner:	Derbi, Nacional Motor SA, Barcelona, Spain

Honda NSR500

The 1985 version of NSR placed fuel and exhausts in conventional position

One of the original NSR500's principal drawbacks becomes apparent on its début at Daytona in 1984: lack of accessibility. Mechanic George Vukmanovich risks second-degree burns as he gropes through the exhaust pipes to reach the spark plugs for a mixture check. Freddie Spencer and chief technician Erv Kanemoto look on. Anyone got the first-aid kit?

The 1985 chassis was strong and simple, with unconventional, slightly undersquare, cylinder dimensions of 54 × 54.5 mm keeping engine width to the minimum. Weight distribution was 55/45 per cent static, without rider. Showa suspension makes much use of titanium and magnesium to reduce overall and unsprung weight. Note the special twin-choke Keihin carbs

Honda's first two-stroke GP bike was the NS500 triple which took Freddie Spencer to GP prominence and both his and the factory's first 500 cc world title in 1983, a year after its introduction. But though the V3 engine's reed-valve induction was to set the style for GP bikes of the immediate future, there were limits to the engine's inherent capacity to produce outright power, and crankshaft vibration problems placed a question mark over reliability when stressed.

Accordingly, Honda came up with a completely new bike for the 1984 season, the NSR500. A true V4, with single crankshaft and reed valves again, it followed the general architecture of the home-built Italian Paton of ten years before but, thanks to HRC's resources, to vastly greater effect. However, in-

fluenced by the design of the ELFe, Honda designed the new machine with the fuel tank under the engine and exhausts above, leading to problems with heat and handling which proved the undoing of lead rider Spencer on more than one occasion. Lawson regained the world title for Yamaha in consequence.

For 1985 the NSR500 was therefore completely redesigned in more conventional form, still with an ultra-powerful engine but now in a Honda version of the Kobas/Deltabox-type frame, with the engine moved further forward and the head angle steepened. Spencer not only won back the 500 cc title, but also took the 250 crown with the NSR250, effectively one-half of the V4 engine in a similar chassis.

Honda, though, suffered another reverse in 1986,

Bolted-up Comstar rear wheels came in both alloy and carbon-fibre versions on the 1985 bike. Early fears about carbon wheels (a result of Spencer's 1984 crash in practice for the South African GP) have been dispelled by exhaustive testing

when a crippling arm injury sidelined Spencer for most of the season, leaving Wayne Gardner generally alone to combat the challenge of five Yamaha V4 riders on the singleton updated NSR500, whose power characteristics and handling were not to the Australian rider's liking. He finished second in the championship; for 1987, an entirely new bike was in order.

Ignition and water-pump were driven off a small secondary shaft at the crankshaft ends, since the perfect primary balance of the 90-degree cylinder layout meant a balancer shaft could be dispensed with. The engine has only five main bearings, and therefore less inherent friction than the Yamaha, which has eight. Ignition is an OKI computerized electronic system, first used on this 1985 NSR

Spencer in action during the 1985 German GP at
Hockenheim. Tyre problems and the demon wet-
weather riding of Christian Sarron meant he didn't
win this one. But what's one battle, when you end
up winning the war? Note the lack of direct
cigarette advertising, dictated by a German ban
on such: millions of TV viewers could not have
told the difference

Elegant simplicity of design is apparent here, but looks are deceptive. Compare this 1985 model with the 1986 version on page 67

Honda NSR500

Engine:	90-degree V4 reed-valve water-cooled single-crankshaft two-stroke with mechanically-controlled ATAC variable exhaust volume on each cylinder
Bore × stroke:	54 × 54.5 mm
Capacity:	499 cc
Output:	144 bhp at 11,500 rpm
Carburation:	Two 34 mm twin-choke Keihin carburettors
Ignition:	OKI electronic
Gearbox:	Six-speed
Clutch:	17-plate dry (eight friction/nine steel)
Chassis:	Twin-spar beam frame in reinforced extruded aluminium
Suspension:	Front: 43 mm Showa telescopic forks with TRAC brake-operated hydraulic anti-dive in each leg
	Rear: Pro-Link monoshock with single Showa unit
Wheelbase:	1370 mm
Brakes:	Front: Two 310 mm Nissin discs with four-piston calipers
	Rear: One 210 mm Nissin disc with two-piston caliper
Tyres:	Front: 13/60 × 16 in. Michelin radial slick
	Rear: 18/67 × 17 in. Michelin radial slick
Weight:	119 kg dry
Top speed:	Over 300 km/h
Year of manufacture:	1985
Owner:	Honda Racing Corporation, Tokyo, Japan

Above

The 1986 NSR500C saw its engine moved one inch (25 mm) further forward still and chassis construction tidied up. Weight was still practically the same, at 119 kg, give or take a few grams

Right

Different bike, different livery. HRC colours on the factory's 1986 control bike, raced by Keijo Kinoshita to the Japanese title. In Europe, the Yamahas reversed the decision in GPs

Honda NSR500C

Engine:	90-degree V4 reed-valve water-cooled single-crankshaft two-stroke with mechanically-controlled ATAC variable exhaust volume on each cylinder
Bore × stroke:	54 × 54.5 mm
Capacity:	499 cc
Output:	152 bhp at 11,800 rpm
Carburation:	Two 34 mm twin-choke Keihin carburettors
Ignition:	OKI electronic
Gearbox:	Six-speed
Clutch:	17-plate dry (eight friction/nine steel)
Chassis:	Twin-spar beam frame in reinforced extruded aluminium
Suspension:	Front: 43 mm Showa telescopic forks with TRAC brake-operated hydraulic anti-dive in each leg
	Rear: Pro-Link monoshock with single Showa unit
Wheelbase:	1370 mm
Brakes:	Front: Two 322 mm Nissin discs with four-piston calipers
	Rear: One 200 mm Nissin disc with two-piston caliper
Tyres:	Front: 3.25/4.50 × 17 in. Dunlop cross-ply
	Rear: 3.70/7.20 × 18 in. Dunlop radial
Weight:	119 kg with oil/water, no fuel
Weight distribution:	54/46 per cent
Top speed:	Over 300 km/h
Year of manufacture:	1986
Owner:	Honda Racing Corporation, Tokyo, Japan

The true nature of engine layout becomes apparent in this shot of the NSR500C. Relax — it's not a W6! What looks like a third set of cylinders is in fact the reed-valve inlets to the crankcase. A much neater exhaust layout is also conspicuous. Huge 320 mm Nissin brake discs and four-pot calipers provide great stopping power. Note also the deep vee on the radiator, to allow for fork deflection. The TRAC brake-operated anti-dive system in 43 mm Showa forks could be removed on occasion to save almost one kilo in weight

Yamaha YZR500 OW81

When Yamaha quietly switched to reed-valve induction in the middle of their 1984 500 cc world championship season, it was an implicit admission that their bitter Honda rivals were right in bucking the hitherto almost universal disc-valve trend in the blue-riband GP class. But that the lesson should have been taught and learnt that way round was itself surprising, for Yamaha themselves were the earliest protagonists of reed valves on GP two-strokes, especially on their TZ750 which dominated the biggest world title category in the 1970s to the point of killing it off.

Just as the gradual power delivery offered by reeds had tamed the big TZ's fearsome output, so it did the comparable horsepower which by 1984

Aluminium Deltabox frame harnessed the 142 bhp delivered by the twin-crank V4 engine superbly. Twin crankshaft centre covers can be seen just in front of the clutch. Cylinders are disposed at 70 degrees, compared to 50 degrees of the 1984 bike, originally designed as a disc-valver. This gave increased reed-valve area

was delivered by Yamaha's GP 500, with one-third smaller displacement. In fact, Yamaha ran their twin-crankshaft V4 (sometimes pedantically termed a W4) with both disc- and reed-valve induction for a time, but by the end of Eddie Lawson's first title-winning season, had switched right over to reeds.

Honda fought back in 1985, the year that Christian Sarron took his Sonauto OW81 Yamaha to victory at a wet Hockenheim to break the three-year stranglehold by US riders on 500 GPs. A slight power advantage and the brilliant riding of Freddie Spencer was enough to counteract the Yamaha's undoubted handling advantage, occasioned by steady development of the Kobas-type Deltabox chassis.

On the outside there appeared little difference between the 1986 OW81/B and its predecessor, but inside there had been substantial increases in power output, from 142 bhp in 1985 to well over 150 bhp in 1986. Yet the Deltabox frame was well able to meet the demands of the first 150 bhp-plus half-litre, and Lawson's smooth but deceptively fast riding clinched another world title for the sign of the tuning forks — Yamaha's emblem.

Yamaha OW81

Engine:	Twin-crankshaft water-cooled V4 reed-valve two-stroke with variable port timing by electrically-operated power valve		with Öhlins suspension unit operated by rocker arms
		Wheelbase:	1400 mm
Bore × stroke:	56 × 50.6 mm	Steering head angle:	24.5 degrees
Capacity:	498 cc	Brakes:	Front: Two 320 mm Brembo floating discs with four-piston Brembo calipers
Output:	142 bhp at 12,000 rpm (claimed)		
Carburation:	Two 38 mm twin-choke flat-slide Mikuni		Rear: One 220 mm Yamaha disc with twin-piston Yamaha caliper
Ignition:	CDI	Tyres:	Front: 12/60 × 16 in. Michelin radial on Marvic 3.50 in. wheel
Gearbox:	Six-speed		
Clutch:	Multiplate dry (nine friction/eight steel)		Rear: 18/67 × 17 in. Michelin radial on Marvic 5.50 in. wheel
Chassis:	Fabricated alloy twin-spar with welded-on sub-section	Weight:	115 kg with water/oil, no fuel (claimed)
Suspension:	Front: 41 mm Yamaha telescopic forks with no anti-dive	Top speed:	Over 300 km/h
		Year of manufacture:	1985
	Rear: Fabricated alloy swing arm	Owner:	Sonauto Yamaha, Paris, France

Left
A 1400 mm (55 in.) wheelbase was par for a 500 and contributed to Yamaha's excellent behaviour in fast, sweeping turns. Head angle could be adjusted over a range of three degrees, but Sarron's favoured 24.5-degree angle, coupled with 100 mm trail, was conservative by standards of US riders

Right
Ohlins rear suspension unit was near-faultless, according to Kenny Roberts — he should know. 1985 was the first year for Michelin's 17 in. rear and 16 in. front radials

Below
Lawson's 1986 title-winner sported both altered seat and fairing, to allow more room for sponsorship, and a slightly revised rear suspension linkage. The really tricky stuff was

inside. Forks of 41 mm saved weight by opting for twin-rate damping instead of the anti-dive system. The bike scaled 118 kg

Yamaha OW81/B

Engine:	Twin-crankshaft water-cooled reed-valve two-stroke with variable port timing by electrical power valve	*Wheelbase:*	1400 mm
		Steering head angle:	24.5 degrees
Bore × stroke:	56 × 50.6 mm	*Brakes:*	Front: Two 320 mm Brembo floating discs with four-piston Brembo calipers
Capacity:	498 cc		
Output:	145 bhp at 12,000 rpm (claimed)		
Carburation:	Two 35 mm twin-choke flat-slide Mikuni		Rear: One 220 mm Yamaha floating disc with Nissin caliper
Ignition:	CDI	*Tyres:*	Front: 12/60 × 17 in. Michelin radial
Gearbox:	Six-speed		
Clutch:	Multiplate dry (nine friction/eight steel)		Rear: 18/67 × 17 in. Michelin radial
		Weight:	118 kg with water/oil, no fuel
Chassis:	Fabricated alloy twin-spar Deltabox	*Top speed:*	Over 300 km/h
Suspension:	Front: 41 mm Yamaha telescopic forks with no anti-dive	*Year of manufacture:*	1986
		Owner:	Yamaha Motor, Iwata, Japan & Marlboro Team Agostini, Bergamo, Italy
	Rear: Fabricated alloy swing arm with Öhlins monoshock		

Left
Lockheed brakes were fitted to the Agostini team bikes for the last GP of the season at San Marino, in an effort to shake Brembo up: a caliper is just visible in the bottom left-hand corner of the photo. Compare this with page 71 to see how little the bike has changed externally; inside, power was up to around 155 bhp, according to Honda's comparison with their NSR in 152 bhp form. Yamaha said nothing — they just went on winning

Below
Lawson's fluid, graceful style belied how hard he was riding. Yamaha's main advantage was in smooth power delivery and safe handling. It did need some effort to steer into corners, though, perhaps a factor of the longish wheelbase and 24-degree head angle

Heron Suzuki

After a disastrous 1983 season in which they experienced severe handling problems with the flimsy alloy chassis fitted to their factory-supplied XR40 square-fours, the British Heron Suzuki team decided to turn a completely new page in 1984. Designer Nigel Leaper was recruited to produce the first-ever 500 cc GP two-stroke chassis utilizing CIBA-Geigy's aluminium honeycomb material, whose remarkable stiffness-to-weight ratio had already been proved in the racing car world.

The first Heron Suzuki appeared in mid-1984, utilizing an XR40 engine and aluminium facing to

Left
Chassis was light but strong, and engine accessibility unimpaired. Getting the paint to stay on was a bit of a problem, though

Below
Square-four Suzuki engine was tailor-made for Leaper's box-type chassis and M-Board material. Undertray was bolted on to increase rigidity

Left
First Heron Suzuki set the trend towards reducing overall size and increasing stiffness-to-weight ratio by use of CIBA-Geigy honeycomb material for chassis, in spite of fitment of many components from team's stock of Suzuki factory machines. Wheelbase was long at 1430 mm (56 in.), though, and the rear wheel still 18 in.

the honeycomb, which was painted white. GP débutant Rob McElnea gave the bike an encouraging début after early testing by the experienced Stu Avant, but with only 122 bhp available from the obsolescent engine, the bike was down on horsepower compared to the Yamaha/Honda opposition, in spite of the tuning skills of engine-man Martyn Ogbourne.

For 1985, the team went the whole way, selecting carbon-fibre facing for the CIBA-made Aeroweb M-Board, and slashing weight to less than 120 kg. With 131 bhp now on tap from the uprated XR45 disc-valve Suzuki engine, this reduced McElnea's power deficit and thanks to some brilliant riding he was able to utilize the attributes of the little, light bike's handling department to get on terms with the more powerful V4s. Ninth place in the championship was hardly a just reward for the hard work by all concerned, though it did overshadow the factory-backed Gallina Suzuki team and their ill-handling Japanese-built frames. But even with more powerful XR70 engines available from mid-season, the Heron was still down on power and suffered, moreover, from the lack of torque inherent in a disc-valve engine.

McElnea's efforts had promoted him to a ride on a works Yamaha, but his replacement, pint-sized Australian Paul Lewis, was brave if inexperienced and of ideal physical size to further capitalize on the Heron's light weight. A reed-valve factory conversion for the increasingly sophisticated carbon/honeycomb chassis offered increased flexibility and a little more power, but it wasn't until new recruit Niall Mackenzie stunned the racing world by qualifying the Heron on the front row for the last GP of the season, San Marino, that the Heron's potential was fully realized. Coincidentally, Suzuki chose that race to unveil their new V4, opening new vistas for the avant-garde Heron design concept.

With fairing fitted it was hard to tell 'White' Heron from a standard Suzuki. The bike handled surely, braked superbly

Heron Suzuki 500

Engine:	Disc-valve square-four water-cooled two-stroke
Bore × stroke:	56 × 50.2 mm
Capacity:	495 cc
Output:	123.5 bhp at 12,200 rpm
Carburation:	Four 38 mm Mikuni
Ignition:	Nippondenso CDI
Gearbox:	Six-speed
Clutch:	14-plate dry (seven sintered bronze/seven steel)
Chassis:	Bonded Aeroweb (honeycomb/composite material) semi-monocoque tub
Suspension:	Front: 40 mm Kayaba forks with brake pressure-operated hydraulic anti-dive Rear: Full Floater rocker arm system with single White Power unit and triangulated alloy swing arm running on needle roller bearings
Wheelbase:	1430 mm
Brakes:	Front: Two 310 mm steel discs with four differential piston Lockheed calipers Rear: One 210 mm carbon-fibre disc with Lockheed caliper
Tyres:	Front: 13/60 × 16 in. Michelin cross-ply slick Rear: 18/67 × 16 in. Michelin cross-ply slick
Weight:	Not available
Top speed:	285 km/h
Year of manufacture:	1984 with uprated 1982 engine
Owner:	Heron Suzuki Racing, Croydon, Surrey, England

Heron Suzuki TSR 05

Engine:	Disc-valve square-four water-cooled two-stroke
Bore × stroke:	56 × 50.6 mm
Capacity:	497 cc
Output:	131 bhp at 12,500 rpm
Ignition:	Hitachi CDI
Gearbox:	Six-speed
Clutch:	17-plate dry (nine/eight)
Chassis:	Open box-type in carbon-fibre faced honeycomb composite with alloy swing arm and engine as semi-stressed unit
Suspension:	Front: 43 mm Kayaba forks with hydraulic anti-dive Rear: Rising-rate monoshock with White Power unit
Wheelbase:	1400 mm
Steering head angle:	26 degrees
Brakes:	Front: Two 310 mm Suzuki discs with Lockheed four-piston calipers Rear: One 210 mm Lockheed carbon-fibre disc with single-piston caliper
Tyres:	Front: 13/60 × 16 in. Michelin radial on Campagnolo wheel Rear: 18/67 × 17 in. Michelin radial on Campagnolo wheel
Weight:	115 kg dry
Top speed:	295 km/h
Year of manufacture:	1985
Owner:	Heron Suzuki Racing Team, Crawley, Sussex, England

Nigel Leaper walks the 1985 version, the first with a carbon-fibre facing to the honeycomb, back to the pits at Oulton after a plug chop in practice. Note the hoses for hydraulic anti-dive on the front forks

The 'Black' Heron Suzuki, now fitted with XR70
engine in the summer of 1985. Power is up, weight
is down, the 16 in. Michelin front radial is
complemented by a 17 in. rear, and wheelbase is
reduced to 1400 mm (55 in.); frontal aspect is
reduced also. Rear brake disc is in carbon, too,
with AP-Lockheed calipers front and rear

One of the most distinctive colour schemes in motorcycle sport. Skoal Bandit was introduced to bike racing by Heron PR-wiz Garry Taylor. Note the wide-spread handlebars, favoured by rider Rob McElnea

83

Rob Mac at Silverstone in 1985. His broad frame emphasizes the small size of the Heron

For 1986, Suzuki produced the ultimate
development of the decade-old square-four
engine that had earned them four world titles. This
is the reed-valve XR70RV, which initially proved
reluctant to rev until experiments with air boxes for
the side-facing Mikuni carbs resolved the
problem. White Power inverted forks have
replaced the conventional Kayabas used hitherto

On the 1986 Heron, weight was down to 115 kg, easily the lightest four-cylinder GP bike, though some way off the hard-to-attain 100 kg class limit. The edge of one of the reed-valve boxes can just be discerned. Needless to say, the air box uses carbon fibre, too!

Once the problem with carburation had been resolved, the XR70RV was significantly better than its disc-valve predecessor. Yet riders were still left struggling for speed down the straights, thanks to a 15 bhp deficiency and more against the V4s. Only the incredible cornering ability of the chassis and Niall Mackenzie, on a tight circuit like Misano, could redress the balance

Heron Suzuki XR70RV

Engine:	Reed-valve water-cooled square-four two-stroke
Bore × stroke:	56 × 50.6 mm
Capacity:	497 cc
Output:	135 bhp at 12,500 rpm
Carburation:	Four 36 mm Mikuni
Ignition:	Hitachi CDI
Gearbox:	Six-speed
Clutch:	17-plate dry (nine metal/eight friction)
Chassis:	Open box-type in carbon-fibre faced honeycomb composite with alloy swing arm and engine as semi-stressed unit
Suspension:	Front: 54 mm White Power inverted telescopic forks Rear: Rising-rate monoshock with White Power unit
Wheelbase:	1400 mm
Steering head angle:	23.6 degrees (as tested)
Brakes:	Front: Two 310 mm Suzuki discs with Lockheed four-piston calipers Rear: One 210 mm Lockheed alloy disc with twin-piston caliper
Tyres:	Front: 12/60 × 16 in. Michelin intermediate Rear: 18/67 × 17 in. Michelin radial slick
Weight:	115 kg dry
Year of manufacture:	1986
Owner:	Skoal Bandit Heron Suzuki Racing Team, Crawley, Sussex, England

Black is beautiful. The Heron was definitely the best-looking and best-finished of the 1986 GP crop

90

Bimota

Federico Martini (right, with beard) poses with Bimota boss Giuseppe Morri and a brace of DB1 Bimotas. Left is the TT1 Ducati-engined racer, and on the right the road bike prototype developed from it

Tesi 1 at rest in the Bimota factory lobby. Note the horizontal position of the front Marzocchi suspension unit, in contrast to subsequent versions

By a combination of superlative styling, sound engineering, close attention to detail and clever marketing, the name of Bimota has become a byword for motorcycling excellence — at a price. The products of the small Italian company have had an influence on two-wheeled design all over the world, far out of proportion to its relatively small annual production, over the past decade, and appear likely to continue to do so in the future.

Chief design guru of Bimota was formerly co-founder Massimo Tamburini, but during a serious

Tesi 2 used the RS750R Honda factory engine, but problems with the exhaust pipes and camshafts supplied meant the powerband was unexpectedly narrow and hampered development. Its frame is built from carbon-faced alloy honeycomb by Alfa Romeo F1 turbo chassis constructors. The front Marzocchi unit is now vertical, using a similar linkage to the rear. The diaphragm and gas cylinder for a back-up steering system are positioned away from any engine heat, at the rear on the right

illness in 1983 he left the Rimini firm and, after a short spell at the Team Gallina race shop, joined Cagiva to work on their road bikes. His replacement at Bimota was the youthful Federico Martini, who has since not only proved even more prolific than his predecessor, but equally influential.

Martini's first design for Bimota was the startling Tesi project bike, star of the 1983 Milan Show where it was unveiled to the public. Incorporating a carbon-fibre and alloy honeycomb chassis in which to house its 400 cc V4 Honda road engine, the Tesi's great innovation lay in its hydraulically-controlled, hub-centre steering with a single swing arm on each side of the front wheel. This theme was swiftly developed into an endurance bike, powered by a factory Honda

Above
'Steering column' was bolted to the top of the semi-monocoque chassis

Right
Opposed front swing arms gave improved steering-lock compared to the ELF-type parallel arm design. The lower cylinder for the hydraulic steering system is visible behind the suspension upright

RS750R engine, which in 1984 took part in a couple of races as part of its continuing development.

Further work on the Tesi was suspended for a while in 1985, while Bimota fought their way out of a cash crisis that left the company temporarily in the hands of the receiver. One new model resolved the difficulty: Martini's DB1 Ducati Pantah-engined 750 twin which proved a worldwide best-seller for such an expensive machine, and also to be highly competitive on the track. But, certain that the Tesi project was equally vital to Bimota's long-term health, Martini persevered with it and at the 1985 Milan Show revealed the Tesi 3, now with less costly tubular steel chassis and revised front suspension. For the first time, one could see how such a machine could be developed for road use.

At the same time, the need to be competitive with the Japanese works machines in TT F1 racing on which much of Bimota's reputation was built, led Martini to design the FZ750 Yamaha-engined YB4. This first appeared in the summer of 1986 and seemed certain to presage a new Bimota road model on similar lines, at a later date.

Right
Riding the Tesi was an unnerving experience, due to its sudden transition from understeer to extreme oversteer. Unsuitable tyre profile was a possible cause

Below
The ultimate alternative motorcycle? Yet it ran, and could be raced, though there was a long way to go before it could be productionized

Left
Tesi 3 featured a completely new front-end design, with altered linkage and internal wheel kingpin

Below
Tesi 3 had a tubular steel frame, as the next step along the road to a street version. The overall design is shown clearly here, especially the suspension linkage which offered a rising rate, both front and rear

Below right
Bimota bodywork has always been an inspiration to other designers and that fitted to Tesi 3 was no exception

Bimota 750 Tesi 2

Engine:	90-degree dohc V4 water-cooled four-stroke		Rear: Swinging fork with vertical monoshock
Bore × stroke:	70 × 48.6 mm	Wheelbase:	1380 mm
Capacity:	748 cc	Brakes:	Front: Two 300 mm fixed Brembo discs with floating four-piston calipers
Output:	128 bhp at 12,800 rpm		
Carburation:	Four 36 mm Keihin CV		
Ignition:	Kokusan-Denki CDI		Rear: One 280 mm fixed Brembo disc with floating two-piston caliper
Compression ratio:	11.2:1		
Gearbox:	Five-speed	Tyres:	Front: 120/70 VF 16 in. Pirelli radial
Clutch:	15-plate all-metal oilbath multiplate with hydraulic action		
Frame:	Carbon-fibre skinned alloy honeycomb spar employing engine as semi-stressed member, with hydraulic steering		Rear: 170/60 VR 17 in. Pirelli radial
		Weight:	170 kg with oil/water, no fuel
		Top speed:	160 mph
		Year of manufacture:	1984
Suspension:	Front: Swinging fork with vertical monoshock	Owner:	Bimota SpA, Rimini, Italy

Below
With Kobas-type chassis made from Peraluman aircraft alloy, the YB4 represented a new departure for Bimota and Martini, who hitherto had always used tubular steel chassis, except on the early Tesis. Note the specially-cast magnesium sump, to permit the engine to be located low down, yet still allow room for the exhausts

Right
Marzocchi suspension front and rear, as with most Martini Bimotas. The U-frame is the only practicable type of chassis for the downdraught FZ750 engine, as Harris and Yamaha themselves would both agree. Martini originally hoped to build a monocoque design, with fuel carried in the area behind the carbs, but was forced to abandon the idea when he could only find room for 16 of the 24 litres permitted by TT F1 regulations

Right
A sign of excellence: the Ferrari of motorcycles?

Bimota YB4

Engine:	Water-cooled dohc transverse in-line 20-valve four-cylinder four-stroke
Bore × stroke:	68 × 51.6 mm
Capacity:	749 cc
Output:	115 bhp at 11,000 rpm (kit engine)
Carburation:	Four 34 mm Mikuni
Ignition:	CDI
Compression ratio:	11.2:1
Gearbox:	Six-speed
Clutch:	Multiplate oilbath
Chassis:	Aluminium twin-spar beam frame
Suspension:	Front: 41.7 mm Marzocchi M1R telescopic forks Rear: Rising-rate monoshock with fabricated alloy swing arm and single Marzocchi unit
Wheelbase:	1420 mm
Brakes:	Front: Two 320 mm Brembo discs with four-piston calipers Rear: One 230 mm Brembo disc with Brembo caliper
Tyres:	Front: 12/60 × 16 in. Michelin slick on Marvic wheel Rear: 18/67 × 16 in. Michelin slick on Marvic wheel
Weight:	168 kg with oil/water/starter
Top speed:	160 mph
Year of manufacture:	1986
Owner:	Bimota SpA, Rimini, Italy

Few bikes can have handled as well straight off the drawing-board as the YB4. This was only its second visit to a track

Honda TT F1

Above
*Undressed, the RS850R looked deceptively normal
— only Dunlop's world championship winner
sported an alloy chassis that year. At 170 kg dry,
the water-cooled Honda was lighter than most of
the air-cooled 1-litre opposition, and with a
1420 mm (56 in.) wheelbase, a little smaller. Note
the oilbath clutch, invariably retained by most F1
Honda V4s. The radiator area was insufficient to
prevent overheating though — Gardner's seat
melted when the temperature shot off the clock
awaiting the start of the world title round at Assen!*

Left
*Wayne Gardner's British title-winning RS850R
poses in front of the pits at Snetterton in late 1983.
Don't believe the scoreboard: in spite of giving
away more than 100 cc to the opposition, the
859 cc Honda won more often than not*

Few machines have ever dominated their class of
racing against the best of the rest of the world as the
V4 Hondas have in the latter days of TT Formula
One. Denigrators of the Japanese factory's super-
professional approach to winning tend to forget that
they alone have supported the category officially
ever since it began in 1977, originally as a means of
keeping the moribund Isle of Man TT as a world
championship event. If not for Honda's consistent
support for a decade and more, both TT F1 and the
TT races would have sunk without trace. As it is, both
are now flourishing, not least because TT F1 has
been perceived by many small manufacturers, such
as Harris, Bimota, Ducati, Bakker and others, besides
the likes of Honda, to be an ideal theatre for the
development of new four-stroke motorcycles for the
street.

Even the reduction in TT F1 capacity from 1000 to
750 cc for 1984 at the behest of the Japanese
manufacturers who are banned from selling large-

capacity bikes in their home market failed to stifle TT F1. Instead, it allowed Honda to turn the tables on their Suzuki rivals, by initiating the line of machines that would make the term 'Vee for Victory' synonymous with the Big H.

For the final year of the 1-litre formula, Honda introduced their first 16-valve, 90-degree V4 race bike, based on the VF750 road engine but overbored to 75 mm instead of 70 × 48.6 mm. The RS850R gave Wayne Gardner the ideal vehicle with which to cement his rise to stardom, though the first of the 750s the following season produced the same horsepower, albeit at higher revs. As might have been expected, it proved cammier than the big-bore bike, but the 1985 RVF750 marked a return to the RS850's mile-wide powerband and seemingly unlimited reserves of torque. Meanwhile, the tubular steel frame of the RS850 had been replaced by a conventional alloy chassis on the RS750, then by the first of the twin-spar Diamond frames on the RVF; for 1986 this was further developed to feature a 'monobrace' single rear swing arm à la ELF.

All these machines had one other thing in common: each conveyed 'Yer Maun', Irish road-circuit ace Joey Dunlop, to the World TT F1 title, and in doing so established a record that will be hard to equal in the future, whatever the direction of the class after the 1988 introduction of the rival Superbike category at world level.

Honda RS850R

Engine:	90-degree V4 dohc water-cooled four-stroke
Bore × stroke:	75 × 48.6 mm
Capacity:	859 cc
Output:	132 bhp at 11,500 rpm
Carburation:	Four 32 mm Keihin CV
Ignition:	Kokusan-Denki CDI
Compression ratio:	11.5:1
Gearbox:	Five-speed
Clutch:	15-plate all-metal oilbath multiplate
Frame:	Full double-cradle steel tubular chassis with alloy swing arm
Suspension:	Front: 41.3 mm Showa telescopic forks with adjustable damping and hydraulic anti-dive
	Rear: Pro-Link rising rate with single Showa unit
Brakes:	Front: Two 310 mm discs with twin-piston Nissin calipers
	Rear: One 220 mm disc with single-piston Nissin caliper
Tyres:	Front: 3.50 × 16 in. Dunlop KR108 slick
	Rear: 3.85/6.50 × 18 in. Dunlop KR108 slick
Weight:	171 kg
Top speed:	171 mph
Year of manufacture:	1983
Owner:	Honda Britain Racing Team, London, England

Left

For the first year of the 750 cc formula in 1984, Honda fitted all their works bikes with alloy frames, saving 10 kg in weight. The front wheel reverted to 18 in. instead of the 850's 16 in. front, largely at the behest of the French endurance team who found it permitted faster brake pad and wheel changes

Below left

Basking in the warm glow of success, the RS750R revealed a worrying propensity to fracture exhaust pipes. Dunlop actually stopped to tear off part of one before resuming his winning way in the IoM TT. The engine liked to be kept revving in five figures

Below

With a year of intensive development courtesy of the US Superbike team, where the 750 formula had been introduced a year earlier, Honda were ready from the beginning in Europe. The engine was largely unchanged outside, though the addition of two extra alloy radiators indicated a concerted effort to address the cooling problems. Cylinders were shaved off the road bike's mock 'fins' in apparent, but trivial, contravention of the TT1 regulations banning alteration to major engine castings. Why bother?

Home . . . Wayne Gardner en route to another British F1 title — he won every round he rode in, including this one at Brands Hatch. Note the rectangular slot in the fairing nose, designed to feed air via an alloy conduit forming the fairing bracket to a still-air box from which the carbs breathed

Honda RS750R

Engine:	90-degree dohc V4 water-cooled four-stroke
Bore × stroke:	70 × 48.6 mm
Capacity:	748 cc
Output:	132 bhp at 12,000 rpm
Carburation:	Four 34 mm Keihin CV
Ignition:	Kokusan-Denki CDI
Compression ratio:	10.5:1
Gearbox:	Five-speed
Clutch:	15-plate all-metal oilbath multiplate
Chassis:	All-alloy square-section tubular duplex cradle
Suspension:	Front: 41.3 mm Showa telescopic forks
	Rear: Pro-Link monoshock with single Showa unit
Wheelbase:	1425 mm
Brakes:	Front: Two 310 mm discs with four-piston Nissin calipers
	Rear: One 250 mm disc with twin-piston Nissin caliper
Tyres:	Front: 3.50/3.25 × 18 in. Dunlop KR124A intermediate on Dymag wheel
	Rear: 3.50/6.50 × 18 in. Dunlop KR135 intermediate on Dymag wheel
Weight:	160 kg dry
Top speed:	165 mph
Year of manufacture:	1984
Owner:	Honda Britain Racing Team, London, England

Left
Dunlop's 1985 RVF750 was the best yet. Engine output was up 3 bhp to 135, yet it was much more flexible than the RS750R. The front wheel was now 17 in.

And away . . . Joey Dunlop and Roger Marshall take their Honda double act to the streets of Vila Real. Marshall won this Portuguese round of the world title and gave Dunlop his closest run yet for the championship. Bad luck at the final round in Belgium proved his undoing, when the normally ultra-reliable V4 engine expired

Above
Honda introduced their new Diamond frame with some fanfare at the Le Mans 24 Hours in April, then suffered the embarrassment of having both bikes retire with broken engine mounts. Sums were redone, and strengthening welded in above the upper cylinders. After that, no more worries: Dunlop won every round en route to a fourth world title

Left
After the slightly finicky RS750R, the first RVF set new standards of four-stroke performance and handling. For some, it was the perfect racing motorcycle. Maximum horsepower was delivered at just 11,000 rpm, but if you insisted you could rev it to 13,000. Not much point really

Below
Overheating was now a thing of the past, thanks to a revised cooling system and two large radiators in place of the RS750R's three. The exhaust system was also new, the four-into-two-into-one design comprising no less than 16 different sections. It didn't break any more, either

Above
Magnesium-bodied Keihin CV carburettors were a constant feature of F1 Honda V4s all along, and vastly expensive. The frame was cleaned up and stengthened for the 1986 season

Above
'Single-sided' rear swing arm saved time in the pits at tyre changes except, ahem, in the opening round at Misano. The main improvement in engine output came from its ability to use round exhaust pipes where they pass behind the engine, rather than the oval ones previously used to clear the swing arm

Right
Dunlop's 1986 title-winner at its home base at Suzuka. Engine power was up slightly, weight was down a little, enough to fend off the most determined challenge yet from Ducati and Suzuki. For the first time in five years Dunlop, and Honda, looked vulnerable

Left
Joey Dunlop about to run out of fuel on the last lap of the first 1986 world title round at Misano, when on the verge of heading Lucchinelli's works Ducati for the first time in the race — maybe. It was Honda's first defeat in the world TT F1 series in almost three years, a measure of their dominance hitherto. But they still won the title for a record fifth time in a row

Above
In spite of the introduction of a new VFR road bike with a 180-degree crankshaft, Honda persisted with 360-degree engines for racing, citing improved power delivery. Ignition on the 1986 RVF was Matsuba electronic, in place of the previous Kokusan CDI

Honda RVF750 F1

Engine:	90-degree dohc V4 water-cooled four-stroke
Bore × stroke:	70 x 48.6 mm
Capacity:	748 cc
Output:	135 bhp at 11,000 rpm
Carburation:	Four 36 mm Keihin CV
Ignition:	Kokusan-Denki CDI
Compression ratio:	11:1
Gearbox:	Five-speed
Clutch:	15-plate all-metal oilbath multiplate with hydraulic operation
Chassis:	Twin-spar beam frame in reinforced extruded aluminium
Suspension:	Front: 43 mm Showa telescopic forks with TRAC brake-operated hydraulic anti-dive
	Rear: Pro-Link monoshock with single Showa unit
Wheelbase:	1395 mm
Brakes:	Front: Two 320 mm Nissin discs with four-piston calipers
	Rear: One 195 mm Nissin disc with two-piston caliper
Tyres:	Front: 3.50/5.10 × 17 in. Dunlop KR106 on 3 in. Marvic wheel
	Rear: 3.75/7.00 × 18 in. Dunlop KR108 on 4.5 in. Marvic wheel
Weight:	152 kg dry
Top speed:	172 mph
Year of manufacture:	1985
Owner:	Honda Britain Racing Team, London, England

By Cosworth,
with a bit of help
from Norton

Ten years separate Ian Sutherland's pair of Cosworth-engined bikes. The original 750 cc Norton Challenge, with twin-shock rear suspension, is on the right, confronting the 1984 Harris-framed Cosworth BoTT racer with engine bored to 825 cc

Above
Harris' chassis consisted of tubular subframes bolted to cambox and rear of crankcases to support suspension components, much as the ELF2 did. The rear unit was a White Power; the 825 cc engine delivered 114 bhp according to Cosworth dyno sheets, running on Lucas fuel injection. Throttle action was very heavy, though

Above right
Twin overhead camshafts were driven by toothed belt up the left of the engine. Ceriani front forks were fitted with Spondon mechanical anti-dive

The Battle of the Twins class, which began in the USA in 1980, has given a new lease of life to many previously obsolescent engine designs, as well as provided a rationale for construction of a host of interesting one-off machines.

Two of the most unusual, as well as the most competitive, such bikes are the two Cosworth-engined machines built in Britain in 1985. The idea stemmed from Scottish enthusiast Ian Sutherland, a Norton fan, who obtained an extensive supply of parts for the abortive Norton Challenge F750 project of the mid-1970s, along with a pair of the prototype bikes which were effectively the last gasp of the moribund NVT combine.

Sutherland entered one of the original Challenge bikes, as raced by Dave Croxford and the like, in British BoTT events in 1983 and was pleasantly surprised to find it quite competitive. Accordingly, he asked F1 racing car engine builders Cosworth who had been responsible for designing the eight-valve, water-cooled, 360-degree parallel twin, to develop it further, ten years on. At this point, one of Cosworth's new owners, Bob Graves, got interested in the project and decided to build his own Cosworth-based motorcycle.

The result was two different but exciting modern British twin-cylinder racers, each of which had their measure of success. Graves' Quantel was the most high-profile, thanks to the efforts of constructor Gary Flood and rider Paul Lewis, an Australian duo who surprised the American BoTT scene with a stirring second place in the 1986 Daytona event, after an early duel with the works Ducatis of Marco Lucchinelli and Jimmy Adamo, and the factory-backed Harley-Davidson, 'Lucifers Hammer'. Sutherland's bike was not raced as much, and sadly never ventured out of Britain, though rider Rob Sewell, who was also responsible for the bike's construction, managed to lap the Isle of Man at just on 100 mph with it — far faster than the original Norton Challenge was ever able to do.

The handling of Harris' chassis was uncertain, thanks probably to an unfortunate combination of a 16 in. front wheel and excessive trail. The bike needed more development, but was promising

Harris-Cosworth P86

Engine:	Water-cooled dohc eight-valve 360-degree parallel twin-cylinder four-stroke		and rear swing arm pivoting on crankcases
Bore × stroke:	90 × 64.8 mm	Suspension:	Front: 38 mm Forcella Italia telescopic forks
Capacity:	825 cc		Rear: Monoshock rising rate with horizontal White Power unit
Output:	114 bhp at 10,750 rpm (at crankshaft)	Wheelbase:	1475 mm
Fuel system:	Lucas fuel injection with mechanical metering system	Brakes:	Front: Two 280 mm Brembo discs
Ignition:	Capacitor discharge electronic system		Rear: One 220 mm Brembo disc
		Tyres:	Front: 3.50/5.00 × 16 in. Dunlop KR106 on Dymag wheel
Compression ratio:	11:1		Rear: 3.85/6.50 × 18 in. Dunlop KR108 on Dymag wheel
Gearbox:	Five-speed with Hy-Vo chain primary	Weight:	180 kg with water/oil, no fuel
Clutch:	Four-plate oilbath with diaphragm spring	Top speed:	160 mph (estimated)
		Year of manufacture:	1984
Chassis:	Tubular steel front subframe with engine as fully-stressed member	Owner:	Ian Sutherland, Forfar, Scotland

Left
Quantel came after the Sutherland bike but was more successful, thanks partly to the sure-footed Exactweld chassis, which used engine architecture to advantage. The cantilever rear end ties suspension forces to the steering head, positioned by bolting the forks to the cambox via sheet metal fabrication. At 173 kg, this bike was no featherweight, but was still 6 kg lighter than the Harris. Heavy engine balance shafts were the culprits

Below
Flood opted for twin 40 mm Amal carbs instead of the heavier and more complicated fuel injection: developed for car use, it was also troublesome at part-throttle openings

Quantel-Cosworth JAB

Engine:	Water-cooled dohc eight-valve 360-degree parallel twin-cylinder four-stroke
Bore × stroke:	90 × 64.8 mm
Capacity:	825 cc
Output:	105 bhp at 10,500 rpm (at gearbox)
Carburation:	Two 40 mm Amal Mark 2 with remote floats
Ignition:	Motoplat CDI
Compression ratio:	11.7:1
Gearbox:	Five-speed with Hy-Vo chain primary
Clutch:	Four-plate oilbath with diaphragm spring
Chassis:	Fabricated alloy front subframe with engine as fully-stressed member and rear swing arm pivoting on crankcases
Suspension:	Front: 40 mm Kayaba forks with hydraulic anti-dive
	Rear: Cantilever monoshock with White Power unit
Wheelbase:	1485 mm
Steering head angle:	26.5 degrees
Brakes:	Front: Two 300 mm floating Brembo discs with four-piston Brembo calipers
	Rear: One 220 mm floating Brembo disc with two-piston Brembo caliper
Tyres:	Front: 11/60 × 18 in. Michelin on Dymag wheel
	Rear: 16/70 × 18 in. Michelin on Dymag wheel
Weight:	173 kg with oil/water, no fuel
Top speed:	158 mph
Year of manufacture:	1985
Owner:	Bob Graves/Quantel Sport, Caterham, Surrey, England

Left
Cobby, complicated yet surprisingly compact, the Quantel may yet turn out to be the ultimate British parallel twin

Below
Paul Lewis sweeps on to the Daytona banking in pursuit of the works Ducatis. His courageous riding and light weight did much to make the Quantel competitive

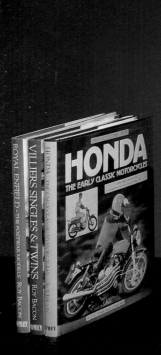

Osprey Collector's Library Backlist

AJS and Matchless — The Postwar Models
Roy Bacon
0 85045 536 7 £8.95

Ariel — The Postwar Models
Roy Bacon
0 85045 537 5 £9.95

BMW Twins and Singles
Roy Bacon
0 85045 699 1 £9.95

British Motorcycles of the 1930s
Roy Bacon
0 85045 657 6 £14.95

BSA Gold Star and Other Singles
Roy Bacon
0 85045 447 6 £8.95

BSA Twins & Triples
Roy Bacon
0 85045 368 2 £8.95

Classic British Scramblers
Don Morley
Foreword by Jeff Smith
0 85045 649 5 £9.95

Classic British Trials Bikes
Don Morley
0 85045 545 6 £8.95

Classic Motorcycle Racer Tests
Alan Cathcart
0 85045 589 8 £8.95

Ducati Singles
Mick Walker
0 85045 605 3 £8.95

Ducati Twins
Mick Walker
0 85045 634 7 £9.95

Honda — The Early Classic Motorcycles
Roy Bacon
0 85045 596 0 £8.95

Kawasaki - Sunrise to Z1
Roy Bacon
0 85045 544 8 £8.95

Military Motorcycles of World War 2
Roy Bacon
0 85045 618 5 £8.95

Moto Guzzi Twins
Mick Walker
0 85045 650 9 £9.95

Norton Singles
Roy Bacon
0 85045 485 9 £8.95

Norton Twins
Roy Bacon
0 85045 423 9 £8.95

Royal Enfield — The Postwar Models
Roy Bacon
0 85045 459 X £8.95

Spanish Postwar Road and Racing Motorcycles
Mick Walker
0 85045 705 X £9.95

Suzuki Two-Strokes
Roy Bacon
0 85045 588 X £8.95

Triumph Singles
Roy Bacon
0 85045 566 9 £6.95

Triumph Twins and Triples
Roy Bacon
0 85045 700 9 £9.95

Velocette Flat Twins
Roy Bacon
0 85045 632 0 £6.95

Villiers Singles & Twins
Roy Bacon
0 85045 486 7 £8.95

Vincent Vee Twins
Roy Harper
0 85045 435 2 £8.95

Yamaha Dirtbikes
Colin MacKellar
0 85045 660 6 £9.95

Yamaha Two-Stroke Twins
Colin MacKellar
0 85045 582 0 £8.95